Could All Religions Be True?

The Short Answer is Yes
Essays from Outside the Spiritual Box

by Jack Preston King

Published by New Paradigm Press

Could All Religions Be True?
The Short Answer is Yes. Essays from Outside
the Spiritual Box

Published by New Paradigm Press

ISBN: 9781793891051

Contents

The Philosophical Problem of Religious Diversity
And the Price Philosophers Pay for Thinking They've Solved It

I was a Teenage Sci-Fi Atheist

Through the age of sixteen, I was a good Methodist boy. I went to church every Sunday, which included an hour of Sunday school before services. I attended weekly youth group meetings. I sang in the choir. I joined the Youth for Christ group at my school (religious clubs in public schools were common in the late 1970s).

Then one day in 1980, about halfway through the Iranian Hostage Crisis, I had this conversation with my mother:

"I'm not going to church anymore."

"Yes, you are." Her tone made clear that her hackles were up and she was ready for a fight. I was sixteen. We'd had a number of tense conversations that year. This may have been the most difficult for her, though, devout Christian that she was.

"I'm serious." I said. "I've thought this all the way through. I don't believe anymore."

"What don't you believe?"

"Any of it. God. Jesus. Heaven. Hell. It's all made up."

"What're you now, some kind of Buddhist?"

At sixteen, I read almost exclusively science fiction. Considering the hundreds of '50s, '60s and '70s sci-fi novels stacked floor to ceiling along the walls of my bedroom, some of them pretty theologically "out there"– Roger Zelazny's *Lord of Light*, Arthur C. Clark's *2001: A Space Odyssey*, Walter M. Miller, Jr.'s *A Canticle for Leibowitz*, Frank Herbert's *Dune,* and many more — it was a fair question. At sixteen, from years of reading science fiction, I knew quite a bit more about the various world religions, numerous otherworldly faiths that existed only in books, and theological questions in general than most kids my age. I thought and talked about religion a lot, though nearly always in a sci-fi context — a holy trinity of God, spaceships, and First Contact scenarios. I felt sure, in my smug sixteen year old way, that I knew a whole lot more about spiritual matters than my small-town-born-and-raised mother.

"Oh, heck, no," I said. "Buddhism's made up, too."

"Well, that's a relief." She almost smiled. Then her eyes narrowed. "People who don't believe in God go to Hell, Jack. You know this."

"That makes no sense to me. If God isn't real, then Hell isn't real, so…"

"Why do you think that? How did you reach this brilliant conclusion?"

My moment in the spotlight had arrived. I was pretty sure I was the first person in the whole history of the world to have successfully solved the "religious problem," and I was ready to preach my newfound atheism from the rooftops. I was the smartest kid on earth! *Yay, me!*

"OK, here's the thing," I said. "Christianity says that God, Jesus, and the Holy Spirit are all the same guy. While we're alive we go to church so when we die we can go to heaven. Buddhists say there is no God, no heaven, and we just reincarnate over and over. Muslims say there *is* a God, but Jesus was just a regular human being, not God. Jews think Christians and Muslims both have God wrong. Hindus have thirty million gods. The ancient Greeks thought Zeus…"

"What's your point?"

"That they're all the same! They're all just stories people made up to feel like they understand the world. But *feeling* like a story's true doesn't *make* it true…"

"Christianity is not *just a story*. The Bible…"

"*The Bible?* How is the Christian Bible different from the Muslim Koran, or the Hindu Vedas, or the Buddhist…?" I couldn't find the word for whatever Buddhists called their scriptures, so I just tapered off.

"*The... Bible... Is... True...*," she said. "That's the difference."

"No, Mom, it's not. It can't be."

Silence. Not doubting silence. Angry silence. She folded her arms across her chest.

"Here's the thing," I continued. "The different religions of the world can't all be true because they contradict each other all over the place. They fight wars over this stuff. If they were all right about God they'd all agree about everything. But they don't. So they can't all be right. The only sane conclusion is that *they're all wrong*."

"What if one of them is right and all the rest are wrong? What if Christianity is right and you wind up in Hell for thinking this way."

I raised my open, empty hands, less in surrender than simply calling off the fight.

"I don't believe it, okay? Isn't it just a whole lot more likely that the whole religion thing is made up? That none of them are true? Either all religions are *right*, or they're all *wrong*. I pick all wrong."

To my sixteen year old genius mind, the religions of the world, lumped together as a whole, were either *all right*, or they were *all wrong*. Religion as a concept was either black or it was white. There could be no middle ground.

Dichotomous Thinking

Twenty-something years ago, as my first marriage was crumbling, I visited a Cognitive Therapist named Margie:

I saw Margie once a week for a year, and learned from her a great many things about the workings of the human mind. Especially helpful was discovering some of the common ways our thinking goes wrong, and learning how to redirect my thought processes when I caught my brain tumbling down an identifiable mental rabbit hole.

One cognitive pitfall causing me a great deal of trouble at the time was *dichotomous thinking*. Here's how Kristalyn Salters-Pedneault, PhD explains the condition on the website *verywell.com:*

Dichotomous thinking, also known as "black or white thinking," is a symptom of many mental illnesses, including borderline personality disorder (BPD). If you have BPD and dichotomous thinking is a struggle for you, you may see only the extremes of things, never the middle. Every thought or situation breaks down to black or white, good or bad, and all or nothing.

One big reason my first marriage fell apart was because I was convinced at that time in my life (late twenties) that there was only one right way to be married, only one right way to live, and only one right way to see the world. "My way" and "the right way" were synonymous terms in my mind. Imagine being married to someone like that. Divorce was probably inevitable.

I'd been thinking that way about just about everything since I was a kid. My religious conversation with Mom at sixteen is a typical example. As a teenager, I was applying to long ages of world religious history, and to the experience of billions of real human believers in every faith, the very same dichotomous thinking that I would later come to recognize as a disordered, marriage-killing plague in my life.

I was thinking about religion in a way that the science of psychology identifies as a symptom of mental illness.

And I was damned proud of myself for doing so.

As a divorced adult (early 30s), I spent a year in therapy working hard to overcome both dichotomous thinking and my misplaced pride in the unfounded certainty it provided. The happy life and great second marriage I have today were made possible by that work.

The Philosophical Problem
of Religious Diversity

So, imagine my surprise, while listening this week to lecture #10, *"Can Mystical Experience Justify Belief?"* in the Great Courses lecture series *The Big Questions of Philosophy*, to hear Professor David K. Johnson offer my teenage, black and white argument as a rational philosophical approach to what he labels *The Philosophical Problem of Religious Diversity*. It's basically an argument against the acceptance of any claim to religious truth, whether that claim is made by an individual based on his or her personal religious experience, or by an organization grown out of the revelatory experiences of religious founders of the past.

The argument goes something like this:

Abraham had a personal vision in which God promised to make him the "father of many nations" and give him possession of the land of Canaan. All of Judaism (and from Judaism, Christianity and Islam) grew like a seed from that vision, fed and watered by the personal revelatory visions of Moses, Ezekiel, Elijah and many others.

The Apostle Paul, a devout Jew, while on the road to Damascus on his way to persecute Christians, was struck by a blinding light that knocked him to the ground. He heard the

voice of Jesus commissioning him to turn from his evil ways and *"...tell foreigners, kings, and the people of Israel about me."* Paul went on to write a significant portion of the New Testament. Much of Christian theology, and especially those doctrines professing that Jesus was the living son of God, and God incarnate in the flesh, are based on his writings.

Muslims believe the Quran was verbally revealed by God to Muhammad through the angel Gabriel, from whom he learned that Jesus was neither God incarnate, nor the Son of God.

Judaism doesn't acknowledge Jesus as divine, or even as a prophet. Islam reveres him as a prophet, but not divine, and believes he ascended alive into heaven. Christians believe he is divine, was crucified, died, was raised from the dead, and only then ascended into heaven. The Mystical revelations received by Joseph Smith, founder of Mormonism, revealed that instead of ascending directly to heaven after the resurrection, Jesus came to America.

Hinduism, Buddhism, Taoism, Shinto and other Eastern religions also spring from the soil of mystical experience, both past and present. They generally disagree not only with one another, but with the Abrahamic religions above.

Throughout the history of our species, objectively similar human religious experiences have resulted in subjectively diverse, and even conflicting beliefs.

For philosophers, that's a problem. *The Philosophical Problem of Religious Diversity.*

Professor Johnson adds that, even if it turned out one of the current world religions was objectively true, we would never be able to identify which one through the use of reason. One religion being right would mean all the others were wrong (because they disagree). And if the majority of religions born of mystical experience are false — which we must necessarily believe if we claim only one among them (our own) to be true — that in itself is overwhelming evidence that mystical experience is unreliable as a source of religious truth. *Most of the time it misses the mark.* And if we're honest, we have to admit that "missing the mark" is just as likely to be the case with our religion of choice as it is with any of the others. It's disingenuous to claim otherwise.

In Professor Johnson's estimation, even if we admit for the sake of argument that we can't know everything, and therefore we can never conclusively rule out the possibility of some divine reality out there that mystical experiences reveal to people, however imperfectly, there remains no way for us to determine which, if any, of those revelations are true. We can't even trust our own religious experience. *Which is functionally the same thing as all such revelations being false.*

It is therefore a wholly rational solution to the problem of religious diversity to defer to the simplest explanation and wash our hands of the whole affair.

They can't all be right, so they must all be wrong.

Shades of sweet sixteen.

The Price They Pay

On the surface, Prof. Johnson's reasoning appears sound.

Yet, I recognize from my year spent in cognitive therapy, followed by two decades of happiness and successful relationships, that his argument is based in disordered thinking. It advances dichotomous, black and white reasoning that allows academic philosophers, and those influenced by their arguments, to feel confident they hold the "one right view" regarding religion, truth, and reality. But the price they pay for that certainty is huge — intellectual and emotional estrangement from billions of religious believers in the world today, and the relegation of thousands of years of human spiritual experience to the dustbin of history.

A human life lived fully, from the earliest days of our species, has always and everywhere included belief in, and interaction with, the supernatural. Long before recorded history, we painted our visions on cave walls, ingested psychotropic plants, and buried our dead with ceremonial provision for the afterlife. Egyptian polytheism lasted more than 3,000 years. Europe was thoroughly pagan for thousands of years before it was gradually Christianized between the 4th and 15th Centuries (it took a long time!). Many Hindus believe their faith predates human origins. It is historically traceable to at least 500 BCE. The roots of Chinese Taoism go back to at least the 400 BCE. For thousands of years before Muhammad, today's Islamic world was predominantly polytheistic.

"Being human" has, always and everywhere, meant, in part, "being religious." Our expressions of religiosity vary with time and location, but the impulse to seek spiritual truth beyond material appearance is constant and universally human.

One important lesson I learned in therapy is that when we demand other people stop being themselves as the price for being with us, that they accept "our way" as the only "right way," *our thinking is disordered*. We are being irrational — and, more often than not, *abusive*.

Mystic visions and religious belief have been integral to the human experience for as long as there have been human beings. Any philosophy that labels this entire rich dimension of human experience "illusion," and the billions of real human beings in all times and places whose lives have been shaped by it, "delusional" is equally irrational. When philosophy is used to shame religious believers (I'm talking about you, Richard Dawkins/New Atheists — and to a lesser, but still noticeable, degree in this lecture, Professor David K. Johnson), it is being abusive, as well.

And we are under no obligation to tolerate abuse.

More to the point, this kind of dichotomous black and white, either-or thinking doesn't actually solve the Problem of Religious Diversity. It only dismisses the question.

So is there a solution? What if followers of just one religion and atheists who reject all religions are both wrong? Are there ways to think about reality in which diverse religious beliefs, even in their conflicting particulars, could all be simultaneously true?

Could All Religions Be True?

Three Mind-Boggling Positive Solutions to the Philosophical Problem of Religious Diversity

The Philosophical Problem of Religious Diversity, stated simply, is that the religions of the world contradict each other in important particulars, including, but not limited to, the existence of God, the nature of God, the number of gods, the role God or gods play in human affairs, and our destiny after death (Heaven? Hell? Purgatory? Reincarnation? Oblivion?). Amidst all those contradictions, how can we know which religion, if any, is true?

Religious believers commonly remain neutral regarding this "problem," accepting their religion of choice as true, while not thinking overmuch about how that judgment reflects on the religions of others. In a civil society, we're taught to respect the right of others to believe as they choose, and people rarely discuss religion in any deep way outside their own faith communities. It's a standard rule of etiquette never to discuss politics or religion in "mixed company."

Atheists propose a negative solution, arguing that contradictory religions can't all be true, and since we can see that most religious beliefs are arrived at by similar processes (personal experience, and first or second hand mystical revelation playing the key role), the logical conclusion would be that *all religions are false*.

Religious believers neutrally choose *one* from the many, while atheists negatively chose *none*.

But are there positive solutions to the Philosophical Problem of Religious Diversity? Are there ways to think about reality in which diverse religious beliefs, even in their conflicting particulars, could all be simultaneously true?

I'll visit three such positive solutions in this essay.

Climbing the Holy Mountain

In college, I minored in Comparative Religion. My favorite professor in that department was a stately gentleman in his eighties, the only teacher on campus who routinely wore a suit and tie to class and lectured from behind a podium. The guy was brilliant. He'd retired from the ministry after two decades as an ordained Lutheran pastor, leading a good-sized big city parish. He'd gone back to school to become a Jungian analyst, and acquired expertise in a wide range of religions, mythologies, and symbols. He practiced that field for another twenty years. Upon his second retirement, he found himself still eager for intellectual challenge, so he signed on as an adjunct professor of religious studies.

He saw all of Humanity climbing the same Holy Mountain. It's a big enough mountain that the landscape and the weather are different depending on which side you're climbing. It's so wide at the base that you have to have ascended quite a distance to even become aware you're on a mountain with more than one side, that you're climbing something other than a flat, vertical plane.

At the top of the mountain is a Great Truth that is calling us all toward it.

Individuals and groups in various times and places have blazed trails toward the top of the Holy Mountain, drawing maps (religions ancient and modern, eastern and western) along the way for their descendants to follow. The maps appear strikingly different for a number of reasons: Because there's more than one way to reach the same destination; Because the diverse cultures, languages and histories of the people making the maps lead them to both experience and describe their journeys differently; Because human spiritual cartographers, being human and therefore fallible, sometimes miss important clues set in their path by the Great Truth calling them from the mountaintop, or they project their desire for such clues where they don't actually exist.

In the professor's opinion, no one had yet reached the top of the mountain, and for that reason, all maps where valuable but unfinished. Every religion had caught and recorded genuine glimpses of the Great Truth at the distant summit. But none would assemble a complete picture until they someday crested the peak.

In the meantime, as we journey up the mountain, everybody's truth, while necessarily incomplete, *is true* from the perspective of the path they're following. He believed that when we eventually reach the top of the mountain, there's no question what we'll find there — *each other*, converging from every direction.

His solution to the Philosophical Problem of Religious Diversity was that, at the summit of the Holy Mountain, apparent contradictions will no longer matter. It's not that we'll find out who was right and who was wrong. Rather, such distinctions will become irrelevant. His go-to "proof text" was the New Testament story where a group of Sadducees tested Jesus with a question about a woman married and widowed seven times on earth — *whose wife would she be in heaven?* Jesus' answer (my paraphrase) was that they'd asked a meaningless question. That's not how heaven works. The professor thought all Great Truth was like that. While we're on one side or another of the mountain, we're stuck with a limited view, and we squabble over particulars. At the summit, that just won't happen, for reasons that will make perfect sense when we get there, but not a moment before.

Of course this is a metaphor, but I think it's a pretty good one. "The Holy Mountain metaphor" positively solves the Philosophical Problem of Religious Diversity by invalidating its first premise — that *religions of the world contradict each other*. It suggests that perceived contradictions are only apparent, the result of drawing short-sighted conclusions before we've gathered all the relevant evidence. When the day comes that we do, in fact, "know it all" (instead of merely pretending to), we'll all agree on everything.

But might there be ways to solve the Philosophical Problem of Religious Diversity that would allow their mutual contradictions to remain contradictions? Are there ways to look at reality in which the statements *"God is one"* and *"God is a Trinity,"* for example, could both be simultaneously true?

Let's keep digging.

Attention Assembles Reality

For several years in my late teens and early twenties, I was obsessed with the books of

Carlos Castaneda. Here's a brief author bio from Wikipedia:

Carlos Castaneda (December 25, 1925–April 27, 1998) was an American author with a Ph.D. in anthropology. Starting with The Teachings of Don Juan *in 1968, Castaneda wrote a series of books that describe his training in shamanism, particularly with a group whose lineage descended from the Toltecs. The books, narrated in the first person, relate his experiences under the tutelage of a Yaqui "Man of Knowledge" named don Juan Matus. His 12 books have sold more than 28 million copies in 17 languages. Critics have suggested that they are works of fiction; supporters claim the books are either true or at least valuable works of philosophy and descriptions of practices which enable an increased awareness.*

I am personally in the "supporters" camp, but only for the totally subjective reason that I loved Castaneda's books, and feel like I got a lot out of them. I have no evidence to present one way or the other regarding their authenticity. When I read his books, I presumed them to be true. If scholars someday prove they were actually fiction, cleverly marketed as spiritual memoir, Castaneda will still have been one helluva smart guy, and his depiction of spiritual reality still impacted a lot of people's thinking in a deep way, mine included.

In don Juan's Toltec cosmology, the universe at large is composed of a more or less infinite number of intertwined energy fields in the form of luminous filaments of awareness. Human beings are also composed, energetically, of luminous fibers of awareness that interact with the universe at large in ways it took Castaneda 12 books to delineate in detail, so I'm not even going to try here.

What matters for this essay is the very basic concept that Toltec shamans understand human beings to be individual bundles of sentient energy floating in an infinite *dark sea of awareness*. Everything we experience as real — the material universe, the earth, human culture, nationalities, our towns, families, and even ourselves, our bodies and minds, everything we know and believe — are a result of where we place our attention. The entire spectrum of human experience inhabits a tiny band of awareness within the ocean of possibility surrounding us, and our personal experience, a much tinier fixed point within that band.

From the moment we're born, first our parents, then eventually everyone around us, education, culture, religion, tradition, etc., train our attention away from the random magical drifting of newborn consciousness toward fixation on a particular spot within the general human band of awareness that people in our

23

time and place define as "the real world." We are taught to "assemble the world" the people around us already live in by having our attention directed to it.

"This is real. That is not. This is important. Disregard that. This is who we are. We're not like that. We always do this. We never do that…"

We're taught the names and uses of objects. We're taught our roles within the family, society, and larger "human reality" as very narrowly defined.

Sometime in the first few years of life, we master our initial lessons, and our attention snaps into place, forming what Castaneda calls the *assemblage point*. By narrowing the focus of our attention to take in only a minute slice of the reality that actually exists around (and within) us, we assemble the world that the people of our time and place agree is real. Most of us will never experience any other reality for the rest of our lives.

But there are other realities.

The spiritual system Castaneda learned from don Juan Matus, which he never labeled "shamanism," but rather *sorcery*, primarily involved the development of a temperament, and the mastery of techniques, that allow one to *move the assemblage point* and experience those other realities. The "ordinary world" we live in is an artifact of having our attention fixed on

24

one point in an endless sea of awareness. Shift that point, and our attention will *assemble other worlds* every bit as real as the "one real world" we were trained as children to perceive.

There's a lot more to Castaneda's metaphysical system, but the few paragraphs above lay sufficient groundwork for the case I want to make in this section.

Castaneda purists, brace yourselves. I'm about to take a giant theoretical leap that would probably give don Juan fits...

1. Let's assume the Toltec description of reality is true.

2. One thing most founders of religions have in common is they report experiences that dramatically defy common consensus reality. Moses and the burning bush. Christ's temptation in the wilderness. Paul's vision on the road to Damascus. Buddha's enlightenment under the Bodhi tree. Joseph Smith's visitation by the angel Moroni, etc.

3. What if extraordinary spiritual experiences like these result from shifts of the assemblage point? What if they defy common consensus reality because they are genuine experiences of *other realities?*

What if religious founders in different times, places and cultures throughout history *experienced other real worlds* every bit as complete and tangible as the one we know — and in those real other worlds, *God is different?* In one world, God is one. In another, God is triune. In a third, God is Goddess. In a fourth, there are many gods.

Thinking of religions as maps, as in the "Holy Mountain Metaphor," what if the particulars of Judaism, Christianity, Islam, Hinduism, Buddhism, Taoism, etc. contradict each other *because they are all working maps that lead to different, yet equally real, destinations?*

It's tempting to posit at this point some version of a *grand cosmic totality* containing all possible worlds, and in which all the apparently conflicting versions of God are reconciled in *"the One True God"*... But it's not necessary to do so for this argument to work. Even if such a grand cosmic totality exists, it would remain the case that all the contradictory spiritual realities referred to by various religions are all equally real, while maintaining their contradictions.

Which positively solves the Philosophical Problem of Religious Diversity.

"But wait!" I hear advocates of logic and reason shouting as they pound tables with angry fists, *"You've added huge, steaming piles of unnecessary entities here! Occam's Razor! Occam's Razor! There is absolutely NO scientific evidence to support this bizarre 'Many Worlds' theory of yours..."*

Or, is there?

The Many Worlds Theory
of Quantum Mechanics

I'm a science fiction writer, not a scientist, so to get this part right I'm going to quote Wikipedia:

*The **many-worlds interpretation** is an interpretation of quantum mechanics that asserts the objective reality of the universal wave function and denies the actuality of wave function collapse. Many-worlds implies that all possible alternate histories and futures are real, each representing an actual "world" (or "universe"). In layman's terms, the hypothesis states there is a very large — perhaps infinite — number of universes, and everything that could possibly have happened in our past, but did not, has occurred in the past of some other universe or universes.*

According to Gismodo.com's website *io9*, one in five quantum physicists, real working scientists who understand logic and make a living from the application of their acute reasoning skills, accept the Many Worlds Theory as a true description of how reality works. Fully 20% interpret quantum theory to require the existence of a ridiculously large number of alternative universes, all slightly different from one another, but all equally real.

I don't want to belabor this point. By all means do your own research. I only want to establish that, right here in the common consensus reality we all share, one in five quantum physicists posit a version of reality that, to my ears, doesn't sound too far removed from don Juan's Toltec cosmology.

Io9 adds a personal spin to their discussion of the Many Worlds Interpretation, suggesting that if the MWI is true, then there are not only an infinite number of worlds out there, there are *an infinite number of MEs*, as well. *An infinite number of YOUs*. One in every world, each different from the you and me reading and writing these words, in some small or large way.

While that thought is plenty mind-boggling in and of itself, I would add for the purposes of addressing the Philosophical Problem of Religious Diversity that what's true for you and me *may be just as true for God*.

Theologians declare that God is *Omniscient* (all knowing), *Omnipotent* (all powerful), and *Omnibenevolent* (all good). If the Many Worlds Interpretation of quantum mechanics is true, we may need to add *Omnidiversa* (all diverse), as well.

What an interesting religion *that* would be!

Diversity as the New Normal

Religious Diversity is only a problem if we accept as given the underlying assumptions that there's only one universe, only one "real reality," and that within that "one real reality," things that contradict each other can never both be true.

All assumptions that stand on shaky ground, if you ask me.

It may be the very nature of existence for contradictory realities to coexist side by side without conflict. The coherence logicians assume as a baseline requirement for their arguments may not only be unlikely, *it may not even be possible.*

In which case Religious Diversity would be our expectation, and could hardly be said to present a "problem."

One More Way All Religions Could Be True

How Spiritual Reality Really Works
My Best Guess, Anyway

Opening Disclaimer

Please note the words *"My Best Guess"* in the subtitle of this essay. I make no claims that any of what follows can be proven objectively. Based on my personal experience, however, I think my hypothesis can be fairly easily verified subjectively by anyone willing to try.

The Problem of Religious Diversity

In my first essay on this topic, *The Problem of Religious Diversity and the Price Philosophers Pay for Thinking They've Solved It,* here's how I explained the philosophical problem presented by contradictions among religious belief systems, quoting my own arrogant sixteen year old self:

"The different religions of the world can't all be true because they contradict each other all over the place. They fight wars over this stuff. If they were all right about God they'd all agree about everything. But they don't. So they can't all be right. The only sane conclusion is that they're all wrong."

The whole point of that essay was realizing now that my sixteen year old self was naïve and jumping to unfounded conclusions, as are philosophers and scientific materialists today who embrace this apparent paradox as proof all religions are irrational, and that religious belief is delusional.

I followed that up with an essay exploring three ways all religions, while maintaining all of their apparent contradictions, could, in fact, be true.

In this essay, I'm going to make one more case for how all the world's religions and spiritual systems — from the most generic, like Moralistic Therapeutic Deism, to the organized world religions, to historically new spiritualties like Wicca, Discordianism, and the New Age movement, in all their cacophonous contradictions — could very well be simultaneously true.

I honestly think this is how spiritual reality really works, way down deep, beneath the surface appearance of things.

Exhibit A: Quantum Jump — Answer to the UFO Mystery

Back in the summer of 1979, when I was a fifteen year old small town science fiction buff, an ad appeared in the classifieds section of *Isaac Asimov's Science Fiction Magazine* for a nonfiction book with the tantalizing title *Quantum*

Jump — Answer to the UFO Mystery. In addition to my love for all things Space Opera, I was crazy about flying saucers, ghosts, psychic powers, and anything to do with fringe science, so of course I sent my dollar (or however much it cost, I don't remember now).

What arrived in the mail was a photo-copied, 28 page booklet by a guy named Peter Simon, expounding his theory that, behind not just UFOs, Bigfoot and mental telepathy, but also every religion since the dawn of time, lay an unseen, all-universe-pervading intelligence he named "The Instructor." The Instructor guides our evolution by manifesting *what we believe about reality*, so that we can test ourselves against it and *evolve beyond our beliefs* toward an increasingly accurate knowledge of reality and Humanity's place and potential within it.

In Peter Simon's view, the religions (and UFOlogists, and psychic investigators) of the world had not so much discovered great, eternal truths about God/Reality, as that The Instructor/God/Reality had, from the emergence of the human species, conformed to whatever shape we chose to project onto it, in order to teach us. It's not that we all along simply saw what we imagined, like dreams or pure fantasy. Rather, what we imagined, The Instructor made real.

Want God to be a burning bush or a pillar of smoke and fire? *No problem.* A trinity? *Check.* Purely monotheistic (not a trinity)? *OK.* A sky god? Mountain god? Sea god? *Check. Check. Check.* Whole pantheons of gods? *Here 'ya go!* Need God to manifest as metallic spaceships and little green men for the age of science? *Will do!*

The notion that reality is a vast spiritual school wasn't a new thought, even back in 1979. The unique twist to Simon's take on the theme, however, was that in his understanding (his *knowing*, he assures readers), The Instructor doesn't conform to our imaginings to show us what is true about Him/Her/It/Reality, but rather *to make us face the absurdity of our concepts*.

Here, Simon is speaking in the voice of The Instructor:

"I'll show you what your brain has created, I'll show you what the brains of those you honor and follow have created, I'll show you part of the childish and insane universe that might result if one starts with a fallacy and overlays it with science and technology, I'll control your mind or your body or your reality if that's what you believe or desire, and then I'll ask you… Does it make sense? Is it consistent? Do you like it? No? What are your conclusions? Who or what do you call for help? Can you think of alternatives? Where do we go from here?"

33

Here's Peter Simon's definition of The Instructor:

I consider it to be the ultimate being, never to this date adequately described by any religion; a teacher of infinite intelligence and practically unlimited power, who can manipulate memory and matter and time and space, which it does for this reason; To demonstrate fallacies to individuals or groups of individuals so that the rest of the pupils in the classroom may observe and decide which notion of the universe and its physical and possibly paraphysical attributes is the valid one.

Scientific materialists, logicians, and other strict rationalists might argue that this sounds a little like a description of what science and logic do — demonstrate fallacies so we can better define what's real. Except, in Simon's view, science, logic, reason, are also masks of The Instructor.

Need God to not exist? *No problem!* Need the universe to be composed of nothing but dead matter you can measure, so you feel more in control? *Sure, why not?* You guys over there want some quantum weirdness to shake things up? *Ta da!*

This little pamphlet had such an impact on me at fifteen that it is sitting on the desk in front of me as I type these words, 37 years, 2 marriages, 11 apartments, and 3 houses later. It may be the only physical object from childhood that I still possess. That's saying something.

Exhibit B: Summoning Forth Wiccan Gods and Goddesses

During my brief first marriage (1993–1997), I followed my wife into the practice of Wicca, and continued on that path alone a couple of years after we divorced. I eventually drifted onto other paths, but I still have a lot of respect for earth based, magickal religions in general, and Goddess religion in particular. I've been something of an amateur theologian pretty much my whole life, so I feel I speak from both knowledge and experience when I say that if you've never invested deep thought into the idea of God as female/feminine, you're missing an important piece of the Divine puzzle…

But that's a topic for another day.

What I want to present in this essay is the Wiccan/occult concept of the *egregore*. It actually goes back to at least Theosophy and the Golden Dawn, but I learned about it through Wicca, so those are the sources I'll draw on here.

In her book *Summoning Forth Wiccan Gods and Goddesses*, Lady Maeve Rhea writes:

Imagine that Divinity is an infinite incomprehensible jewel with an infinite number of facets through which the energy of the Divine is refracted in innumerable ways. In the course of human existence, human beings come into contact with aspects of life that manifest Divinity; its creative power, wisdom, caring. Whether or not they are conscious of it, humans are effected by, and effect, this Divine energy. Then they shape the energy according to their needs — hunting, healing, fertility and childbirth, coming of age, growing old, and finally death — all the things that are basic to human life...

... All of these processes can be better understood and dealt with if there is a way to tap into the Divine energy behind them. Accordingly, what I mean by a God[dess]-Form is the humanly made and defined shape through which a particular aspect of Divinity is made comprehensible to the human mind.

Esra Free, author of *Wicca 404: Advanced Goddess Thealogy*, expands on the basic concept:

Goddess-forms become real because She who is so distant in Her fullness moves willingly to inhabit and speak through the fragmentary forms we create to reflect Her many aspects, just as an actor in an ancient Greek drama might bring to life a specific god or goddess by speaking through a finely-crafted mask. A goddess-form that survives the test of time (Such as Brigid, Persephone, Gaia, Hecate — all the goddesses you read about in "Wicca 101" books) can be seen as a carefully-crafted perfect vehicle, chosen as much by the Great Goddess as by human beings, for expressing a particular fragmentary facet of the Great Goddess's personality, for bridging the gap between the Goddess's desire to share Herself with and know us personally, and our equivalent yearning for conscious communion with Her. In one sense, all the goddess and god-forms, taken together, form a kind of living language in which She speaks to us, and through which we can communicate with Her.

... on the level of personal experience, goddess and god-forms are concretely real entities, with distinct personalities, powers, areas of expertise and concern, quirks of character, etc. In the practice of Wiccan magick, these entities are called egregores. An egregore is a human projection onto the Divine that, over time, becomes real. It is a kind of living answered prayer.

I think what's being said here is remarkably similar in *mechanism*, to Peter Simon's description of The Instructor, though the *intent* differs. Where Simon's Instructor conforms to our projections for the purpose of instructing us, Free's Great Goddess divinizes human projections out of love and mutual longing for relationship. I like Free's version better, because I find the image of Divinity longing for relationship with human beings just as much as we long to know Divinity profoundly moving.

37

Exhibit C: Yaqeen —
Faith in the Idea of Faith

One of my favorite Medium writers, Runjhun Noopur, recently completed a brilliant and inspiring series of essays exploring:

a Sufi Celebration of Life, inspired by one of the most beautiful and poetic languages known to the human kind — Urdu. Urdu is a native of Hindustan or undivided India — one of the 22 official languages of India, and the national language of Pakistan.

One essay in the series focused on the Urdu word *Yaqeen*, which translated literally means "faith." But *Yaqeen* plumbs a much greater spiritual depth than you may have been taught to associate with its English equivalent. Here's Runjhun:

Faith is a spiritual force that surpasses the ideas of religion and God and all other artificial belief systems. Faith is a force of Nature which can be unveiled by the power of our intent. It does not matter who or what do we choose to vest out faith in — our God, this Universe, Life, Ourselves, Passion, Hardwork, Science — because the object of our faith is only incidental. It is the faith that matters; it is the faith that makes for magic and miracles; it is the faith that renders the idea of impossible pointless.

... Faith is the force that activates the Universal consciousness, which then manifests as the form of your choosing. Your God can be as real and tangible as you want Him to be because it is the power of your faith that activates His existence. Ultimately, every manifestation of our faith including the more earthly ones like hardwork or our own spirit or logic or even Science are ultimately a version of the Universal consciousness or that Higher Force that lies at the core of our very being. We all choose to name it differently, and it manifests for us all differently. But it all emerges from our own faith or Yaqeen — the Universal force that threads through us all.

We may be viewing the human/divine equation a bit more from the human side here, but it's definitely the same equation. There is a Universal Consciousness, and there is a Higher Force at the core of our being. In their interaction, God/desses are born.

Exhibit D: Lord Krishna's Universal Form

The *Bhagavad Gita* ("Song of the Lord") is a 700-verse Hindu scripture in Sanskrit that is part of the epic the *Mahabharata* ("the great tale of the Bhārata dynasty"). The bulk of the Gita is a conversation between a warrior named Arjuna and the deity Krishna, the embodiment of the godhead in Hindu theology.

In Chapter 11, at Arjuna's request, Krishna reveals his true, Universal Form:

The Blessed Lord said: My dear Arjuna, O son of Prtha, behold now My opulences, hundreds of thousands of varied divine forms, multicolored like the sea.

O best of the Bharatas, see here the different manifestations of Adityas, Rudras, and all the demigods. Behold the many things which no one has ever seen or heard before.

Whatever you wish to see can be seen all at once in this body. This universal form can show you all that you now desire, as well as whatever you may desire in the future. Everything is here completely.

In the Great Courses lecture series *The Meaning of Life: Perspectives from the World's Great Intellectual Traditions*, Professor Jay L. Garfield explains:

Now comes the theophany itself, the fabulous poetic representation of what the realization of divinity is actually like. We're told that when Krishna revealed himself, "Everywhere was boundless divinity containing all astonishing things. Arjuna saw all the universe and its many ways and parts standing as one in the body of the god of all gods."

Vijayendra Mohanty, in his 2013 Medium essay *Why Hindus Worship Many Gods*, quoted

40

this translation of the *Bhagavad Gita*, Chapter 4, Verse 11:

O son of Pritha! Whoever worships me, in whatever way, I entertain them in that way. Everywhere, men follow along my path.

The god of all gods. In whom *"Whatever you wish to see can be seen all at once in this body."* The Universal divine form which can *"show you all that you now desire."* Who entertains us in whatever way we choose to worship.

This language, to me, sounds very similar to all the previous exhibits. In the Gita's Great Theophany, we see the divine side of the equation stressed, but the human side is there as well. *"Whatever you wish to see,"* Divinity is pleased to manifest, according to our ability, and willingness, to encounter it.

Back to the Problem of Religious Diversity

How could all the religions of the world, which contradict one another in their particulars, nonetheless be simultaneously true?

Consider this. Whatever religion we practice (or don't, hello atheists), we all hold certain ideas about the nature of Divinity in our minds, and, most of the time, we mistake those ideas for Divinity itself.

We're taught the attributes of Divinity in our families, churches, mosques, in books and college courses, etc. Of what we're taught, we remember maybe a third, toss in some wish fulfillment, fear, personal experience, etc., and decide at some point that we understand God (or Goddess, Instructor… you get it). If we're taught or simply choose to believe Divinity doesn't exist, or to make science or logic our God, we mistake *that* for the real deal, as well (it's exactly the same process).

The kicker, in my theory concerning the Philosophical Problem of Religious Diversity, is that the actual *God-Goddess-Instructor-Universal Consciousness-Divinity* out there is cool with whatever image of him/her/it/they we come up with. Divinity — in a divine way, I really don't mean this as casually as it sounds — goes along to get along. *God is not vested in how you or I see God.* That's up to us.

WE EACH CHOOSE THE WAY
DIVINITY MANIFESTS TO US.

Think about that. If you're comfortable with a namby-pamby Moralistic Therapeutic Deism version of Divinity, that's what you'll get. If you're an atheist and, while you're A-OK with medical and technological "miracles," you'd just as soon the supernatural kind stayed out of your sight, that's what'll happen. If you've been taught (and continue to believe; *you can change this*) that God is abusive and angry and wants you in Hell, watch out. Here it comes. If your God is love, welcome to Heaven on Earth. If your God is Goddess, She will be. If you think Divinity is an endlessly fascinating puzzle to be worked, studied and courted for a lifetime (that's me, by the way), *boom!* God is mystery.

No one is right about who/what/where/why/how Divinity really is, in its own self. But no one's wrong, either, when they experience as tangibly real the *God-Goddess-Instructor-Universal Consciousness-Divinity* they believe in.

All religions are true because Divinity does not have a stake in any of our religions being true, least of all in any ONE of them being truer than the others.

WE GET WHAT WE ASK FOR.

WE ARE BEING OBLIGED.

THERE IS POWER IN KNOWING THIS.

That's my hypothesis. Try it on. Test it. See where it leads you. I personally find the idea exquisitely liberating. I imagine others may find it frightening, threatening, or laughable. But hey, that's why I started with a disclaimer.

Are You Spiritual?

If you answered "NO," think again

"The decisive question for man is: Is he related to something infinite or not? That is the telling question of his life." — Carl Jung

Are You Spiritual?

If you answered "NO," think again. Being spiritual *does not* mean you have to:

Believe in God (or any divine beings)

Follow a religion

Be "Saved"

Believe in magic

Have mystical experiences

Pray, meditate, do yoga, "live mindfully."

A lot of spiritual people *do* believe in God(s), follow religions, pursue mystical arts and experiences, and practice mindful disciplines like prayer, meditation, and yoga. *But that's not what makes them spiritual.* It's being spiritual that attracts them to those things.

What makes a person spiritual is not how they view, or don't view, the universe.

What makes someone spiritual is how they view themselves, and by extension, all other human beings.

Are You a Meat Puppet?

There's really only one way to be "not spiritual," and that's to embrace a physicalist/ materialist view of not only the natural world, but also of yourself.

"Physicalism... is the philosophical position that everything which exists is no more extensive than its physical properties, and that the only existing substance is physical. Therefore, it argues, the mind is a purely physical construct." — The Basics of Philosophy

Or as OpenSciences.org's Larry Dossey phrased it in his essay *"Consciousness: Why Materialism Fails"*:

What does physicalism actually look like? ... as astrophysicist David Lindley has said, "We humans are just crumbs of organic matter clinging to the surface of one tiny rock. Cosmically, we are no more significant than mold on a shower curtain." Spirituality, the sense of connectedness with something that transcends the individual self, is equated in this view with self-deception, fantasy or hallucination. In this outlook, meaning, direction, purpose and free will are absent... according to linguist Karen Stollznow, "Thinking is just the meat talking to itself. It's generated by the brain and when we die, unfortunately that dies with us."

Either you view yourself as a crumb of organic matter whose "self" is a brain-generated illusion that will cease to exist at the moment of death, or you hold some kind of spiritual view.

If you believe human beings are more than the meat they're made from, you're spiritual.

That's what "spiritual" means. Everything else is embellishment.

Something More

Once you declare, "I am a physical body *and something more*," you've taken a spiritual stand.

Perhaps you call that *"something more"* spirit. Maybe soul. Maybe just consciousness — a uniquely human consciousness destined to survive physical death.

Maybe you don't call it anything, but your inner experience of your own existence (even Descartes said *"I think therefore I am"*), plus a lifetime of intimacy with other people, tells you that the human *"something more"* is real. That people are more than meat talking to itself, more than mold on a shower curtain. That physicalism/materialism, especially when applied to human beings, is an insulting absurdity.

But, Science Says...

Physicalists/materialists will insist there's no scientific evidence of *"something more,"* so it's delusional to believe in spirit, soul, or even consciousness (there's no such thing as consciousness, according to philosopher Daniel Dennett).

But not even Science holds the physicalist line anymore. Here's Elisa Medhus, M.D., writing in *The Huffington Post:*

... quantum science has begun to steal the show from material science (sorry, Sir Isaac), teaching us that we no longer have to rely on our five senses to hypothesize and eventually define a truth. Just because we can't see, feel, hear, taste or smell something doesn't mean it doesn't exist. As quantum physics comes into its own, studies into the existence of alternate dimensions and consciousness survival after death result in breakthroughs. Not a month goes by that new discoveries aren't becoming breaking news stories: The fact that we may be able to see other dimensions beside our own. The hypothesis that the microtubules in our cell's mitochondria are the origin of consciousness. The idea that our souls may be comprised of tiny subatomic particles known as "neutrinos."

So, Again, Are You Spiritual?

We all experience our *selves*, not just our bodies, to be real. We experience ourselves to be conscious. Most of us, even some atheists, expect our consciousness to continue to exist in some form after death.

That means most of us are spiritual, even if we've never thought of it that way before.

We hold a spiritual view of what it means to be human.

Everything else is embellishment.

What Survives Death?

Your soul is immortal. But it may not be what you think it is.

"Die happily and look forward to taking up a new and better form. Like the sun, only when you set in the west can you rise in the east." — Rumi

Shopping in the Afterlife

A couple of years ago, I found myself in a conversation about the afterlife with a preacher from the local Assemblies of God church in our town. By "conversation," I mean she talked while I listened. Her vision of the afterlife left me speechless.

"In Heaven, the sun will always shine! We'll lounge on white sand beaches drinking fruit juice and laughing joyfully! Then we'll go to golden shopping malls where the shelves are always filled with every kind of wonder, and everything is free!"

Wait, what? Golden shopping malls? Eternal consumerism?

For the record, you won't find anything like her vision of Heaven in the Bible, the newest book of which, *Revelation*, was composed before the year 100. Shopping malls didn't exist until 1956.

What my friend was describing (and projecting as universal for everyone) was a heavenly afterlife *that would make her happy*. That would delight her earthly personality, with its materialistic, shop-till-you-drop tastes.

And she fully expected to arrive there one day, in person, just as she was.

What About Us Survives Death?

Every Christian I've ever known (including me, growing up) at least appeared to believe their *personality* is immortal. That the person they experience themselves to be, on an everyday basis in this one life, is destined to live with God for eternity in Heaven. Their dead relatives will be there to meet them, recognizably the same people they were here on earth — happier, but still the same basic folks. This may not be a theologically sound belief, owing as much to Hollywood as it does to the Bible, but I do think it's a common Christian view of the afterlife.

But is our personality, with all its foibles and failings, desires and dreads, wonders and woe, really what survives death? The part of us most shaped by the outside world? By growing up with our good or bad parents, by what we were or weren't taught in school, by the jobs we've had, opportunities life has offered or withheld, people we've known, TV, the internet?

Are we really destined (or doomed, as the case may be) to remain the person this single earthly lifetime has made of us, forever and ever, Amen?

Atman — Your Soul
is not Your Personality

Not according to Hinduism, where the soul is known as *Atman*.

Here's a definition, from Yogaopedia.com:

Atman is a Sanskrit word that can be translated as "self" or "breath." It is a word that is used in Hinduism to describe the concept of the inner Self. Each person's Atman is regarded as being a part of the universal Brahman [God], which is the eternal Truth or the absolute Universal Principle. ... Atman is seen as being the true Self or Essence of a person.

Digging deeper into why our personalities can't be our souls, here's Mark Berkson, from his Great Courses lecture series *Cultural Literacy for Religion: Everything the Well-Educated Person Should Know:*

So what is the Atman? ... What is the true, supreme self? ... One way to describe the nature of Atman is pure consciousness. *Pure subjectivity. Awareness itself.*

*… When you think of being conscious, you normally think of being conscious **of something**. Conscious of something you see, or taste, or hear. If your Atman is pure subject, then it cannot be an object. So anything that can be an object of your consciousness cannot be it. Since you can be conscious of your body, it can't be your body. You can also be conscious of your thoughts, your emotions, your sensations. Thus none of these is your true self, the pure subject. Take away everything that can be an object of consciousness, and what is left? Consciousness itself… this is your true identity. And that is changeless, deathless, eternal.*

Who Knows?

You can certainly be conscious of your personality. In fact, you probably know yourself pretty well. You've been living with you your whole life. No one knows you like you do.

But ask yourself:

Who is it that knows?

When you know yourself, when you're conscious of your own personality, your likes and dislikes, your memories of who you've been, your dreams for the future, your talents, your yearnings, your fears —

Who is doing the knowing? Who is aware of the personality you usually think of as "I?"

Your Atman. Your soul. The pure consciousness, the awareness itself, that is your true Self or Essence — the witness to all the events of your life, inner and outer, from cradle to grave.

And that's what reincarnates, according to Hinduism.

"As a person sheds worn-out garments and wears new ones, likewise, at the time of death, the soul casts off its worn-out body and enters a new one." — Bhagavad Gita: Chapter 2, Verse 22

At death, your Atman returns to live another life with its own likes and dislikes, memories, dreams, talents, yearning, fears... To witness the travails, from cradle to grave, of a new personality.

But it's still you.

Because you are not your personality. You are your Atman. You are your immortal soul.

Approximate Conceptions

Which remains true whether our souls reincarnate after death or go on to spend eternity with God.

In a 1944 letter, Carl Jung wrote:

53

"What happens after death is so unspeakably glorious that our imaginations and our feelings do not suffice to form even an approximate conception of it."

Whatever comes next, don't expect any golden shopping malls in the afterlife. The personality that cared about such "approximate conceptions" won't be there.

You will.

Are Religion and Spirituality Two Different Things?

A lot of people think so. But is it true?

"A large number of Americans identify as "spiritual but not religious." ...This phrase probably means different things to different people. The confusion stems from the fact that the words 'spiritual' and 'religious' are synonyms." — Robert C. Fuller

Outer Religious Forms

I converted to Catholicism in my twenties in response to a series of spontaneous spiritual experiences I felt were pointing me toward the Church.

Becoming Catholic as an adult requires up to a year of weekly catechumenate classes, and I was glad for the instruction. I was convinced, entering those church basement sessions with a priest and half a dozen fellow converts, that I was about to be handed the Secret Gnostic Keys to Christ Consciousness.

"The Holy Catholic Church!" I told myself, *"Spiritual home of mystics, visionaries, and saints!"*

The priest was friendly, but the dry lessons reminded me of the Methodist Sunday school of my youth. Saints were mentioned (briefly), but mystics and visionaries were nowhere to be seen. The syllabus included 1) The basics of

Christian belief (which I already knew, having grown up Methodist), followed by 2) the structure of the Mass — what the priest does and why, transubstantiation of the host, when to stand, sit, kneel, sing, etc. Between classes, I thrilled to the writings of the mystic Jesuit geologist, paleontologist, and priest Pierre Teilhard de Chardin, who devoted his life to bringing religion and science together, with an emphasis on ecology and Humanity's role in the evolution of the living Earth. I asked about mysticism in my classes, and specifically about Teilhard, but was told, *"Don't worry about that stuff now. Learn the basics. The rest will come."*

"The rest" never came. Life as a confirmed Catholic amounted mostly to a bland repetition of the second half of the syllabus. Stand, sit, kneel, sing. Once a week, for one hour. Wash, rinse, repeat. I liked the priest, but it began to grate on me that his homilies always (and I mean *always*) started with a joke, followed by some lightweight, unchallenging moral lesson, frequently embedded in a story about the St. Louis Baseball Cardinals. Then more standing, sitting, kneeling, singing, followed by a race for the parking lot.

I'd come to Catholicism seeking a larger context in which to frame my spontaneous spiritual experiences. What I found was a frame with no room for my picture. I saw hints of what I thought of as "real spirituality" in the mechanics of the Mass, in high seasonal rituals like the Easter vigil, in Marian devotion. But I could find no one, not in the pulpit or the pews, who shared my mystical view of these things. Instead of a structure that would frame and support spiritual experience, I found a religion that *stood in the place of* spiritual experience. I found good people who seemed content to go through the motions on Sunday morning without digging any deeper. Who seemed unaware that a "deeper" existed.

Practicing Religion
VS Spiritual Awakening

Zen Buddhism was born from a similar observation. Discussing Zen's rejection of most Buddhist religious accoutrements, Mark Berkson draws this analogy in his Great Courses lecture series *Cultural Literacy for Religions: Everything the Well-Educated Person Should Know:*

Imagine a religion that centered around the amazing qualities of mangoes... What if numerous members of the religion spent their time studying the history of mangoes, reading accounts of people who describe the wonderful taste of mangoes, setting up businesses to sell mangoes, and learning the botanical details of the mango — and yet have never tasted a mango? You'd want to shake them and say,

"Put down the books! Stop reading about other people's experiences! Taste the mango! That's all you need!"

Zen's founders saw people practicing Buddhist religious forms, but not becoming Buddhas. Studying sutras and performing rituals *in place of* pursuing enlightenment. They founded Zen as a return to the historical Buddha's original teaching.

Discard outer forms. Experience the mind directly. Awaken.

This is how religion and spirituality are commonly distinguished in the West today. Religion is seen as an outer form (Buddhist, Catholic, or otherwise) that people accept in place of "tasting the mango" of enlightenment, God, soul, awakened mind, Christ Consciousness, etc. Spirituality is seen as dropping the externals and reaching for the mango. A lot of people these days consider religion and spirituality to be mutually exclusive terms.

But is it True?

Can religion and spirituality really be separated like that?

I think the answer is *"NO."* Especially in our scientific, 21st Century Western culture.

Let me explain. Let's stick with Zen as an example.

The word "Zen" is a Japanese trans-literation of the Sanskrit word *Dhyāna* (or *Jhāna* in Pali), which according to Wikipedia:

*...is a series of cultivated states of mind, which lead to a "state of perfect equanimity and awareness (upekkhii-sati-piirisuddhl)." It is commonly translated as **meditation**, and is also used in Hinduism and Jainism.*

Zen Buddhism = "Meditation Buddhism."

***Dhyāna*, or meditation, is a religious exercise**, whether practiced by Buddhists, Hindus, Jains, or anybody. It's a method of pursuing a religious end — *enlightenment*. Zen, with its focus on meditation leading to enlightenment, and its rejection of outer religious forms, is still Buddhism. It might be bare bones Buddhism, core Buddhist spirituality, but it's still fundamentally religious.

How so?

Because the goal of meditation is *enlightenment*, awakening, a state of mind that can only be acknowledged to exist within a religious context. Scientists might image the brains of Zen masters and concede that long term meditation has measurable effects on physical brains. But can you imagine science (as it is practiced today) ever acknowledging *the reality of enlightenment?* Of higher consciousness? Of Buddha-level awakening?

Spiritual but not Religious
— Is that a Real Thing?

Once the Buddha attained enlightenment, he remembered all of his past lives — *more than 500 of them!*

What would science do with a claim like that today?

Acknowledge the reality of past lives and reincarnation? Of enlightenment/awakening?

Or would it work to "explain away" those memories — and Buddha's awakening — as hallucinations? As tricks of the brain?

"Nothing to see here. Move along…"

Buddha's enlightenment and past lives are *religious beliefs.* Taking either one seriously is a religious act. Trusting in the reality of the Buddha's awakening enough to pursue a taste of it for yourself requires religious faith.

In Christian-dominated American culture, people tend to treat "Christianity" and "religion" as synonyms, to use the words interchangeably — and to declare when they reject Christianity that they've rejected religion. Spirituality beyond that point often means adopting Buddhist, Hindu, Taoist, or other non-Christian terminology and methods and labeling oneself "spiritual but not religious."

That's just cultural appropriation. Ask any of the millions of religious Buddhists, Hindus, and Taoists across Asia. Adopting Eastern religious terminology and methods is still practicing religion.

Maybe not one's native or family religion, but religion nonetheless. A label can't change that.

Some "spiritual but not religious" people meditate or practice Hatha Yoga or Tai Chi, all exercises with a religious origin, but only for the physical benefit — to reduce stress, strengthen the body, and focus the mind, with no expectation of tasting higher consciousness.

But can such a secularized approach be rightly labeled "spiritual?"

Healthy living, sure. But spiritual? What "spirit" are they talking about?

What's the non-religious meaning of the word "spirit?"

The words "Christianity" and "religion" are not synonyms.

But "spiritual" and "religious" are.

Because religion is how people everywhere, East and West, categorize and relate to the spiritual dimension of human experience that science can't measure, and which it therefore treats as unreal.

Things like enlightenment, past lives, the soul, God.

We're at this Impasse
Because Science is Stuck

But people really do attain enlightenment. They become Buddhas. They achieve Christ Consciousness. They experience their own souls. They encounter gods, angels, ghosts, nature and elemental spirits. They glimpse heavens, hells, underworlds and otherworlds. They leave their bodies and return in Near Death Experiences (and astral projection). They remember past lives. They speak in tongues. They are filled with the Holy Spirit. They cast spells that work. They have prophetic dreams, and all manner of mystical experiences.

As long as science's remains stuck on the response, *"Meh... No they don't,"* neither science nor religion can move forward. Neither can change because both remain necessary in their current, opposed state.

Science for understanding the natural world.

Religion for fathoming spiritual experience.

I call for the evolution of both religion and science. I see no value in maintaining empty religious forms *OR* scientific dogmas that presume the unreality of the spiritual.

Religion has to "dig deeper," and taste the mango.

Science must reach further, and respond, *"Yeah... Maybe they do."*

Mythology is a Language. It's How Our Souls Speak to Us.

Learn to speak the soul's language

*"A one sentence definition of mythology?
Mythology is what we call someone else's
religion."* — Joseph Campbell

Are We Living in a Post-Mythological Era?

A lot of people think Humanity has evolved beyond the need for mythology. That it's time to be done with religion, to discard all religious mythologies, and forge a common future based on reason alone. God is dead, and the efforts of a superstitious few to resuscitate Him/Her /It/They are holding us all back. The future belongs to science, technology, logic.

Here's how Michael Vannoy Adams describes the basic argument in a talk presented at the "Psyche and Imagination" conference of the International Association for Jungian Studies:

[Psychologist] Wolfgang Giegerich has argued that, at this stage in the history of conscious-ness, ...it is a fallacy to resort to "any ancient mythological figures" in an attempt to account for the modern situation.

... the modern psychological situation is utterly without precedent, without parallel. It is so radically different — or, as he says, so logically different — [that it] ... has "fundamentally broken with myth as such, that is, with the entire level of consciousness on which truly mythic experience was feasible."

... What is the "modern situation?" As Giegerich defines it, it is... the stage of the computer, Internet, cyberspace, and virtual reality. For Giegerich, the modern psychological situation is so technological that it is post-mythological.

The Language of the Soul

This critique of mythology, and every reasoned plea for the abolition of religion that follows similar logic, makes sense if human beings are only what materialist science says we are — physical bodies set in motion by chemistry and the electrical chattering of neurons in our brains.

Giegerich's logic would be inarguable if we were nothing more than our bodies. And if mythology/religion was, in fact, just empty fantasy, a special category of neural chatter.

But I think both of those assumptions are wrong.

We are more than our bodies. We are our souls.

And myth is more than empty fantasy. Mythology is a language.

It's how our souls speak to us.

The Soul's Five Sheathes

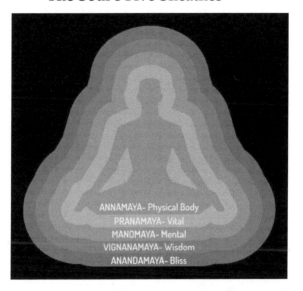

The soul in Hinduism is known as *Atman*. Atman is not our bodies, or our thoughts, or our feelings, or our personalities. Atman is the pure consciousness, the awareness itself, that is our true Self or Essence. It's what's eternal about us, what reincarnates.

The Taittiriya Upanishad teaches that the Atman is enclosed within five *koshas*, or sheathes. They are sometimes referred to as the five bodies or vehicles of the soul.

The highlighted descriptions that follow are from Joseph Campbell's book *Pathways to Bliss: Mythology and Personal Transformation.*

The first, and coarsest, sheath is the *Annamaya kosha*, or "Food Sheath":

"That is your body, which is made out of food, and which will become food when you die. The worms, the vultures, the hyenas, or the flame will consume it."

The second sheath is the *Pranamaya kosha*, or "sheath of breath." It's also commonly labeled the "energy sheath," but Campbell uses "breath," so I'll follow his lead here:

"The breath oxidizes the food. The breath turns it into life. That's this thing, this body — food on fire."

The third sheath is the *Manomaya kosha*, or "mental sheath":

"This is the consciousness of the body, and it coordinates the senses with the 'you that thinks it is you' [ego, personality]*."*

These first three sheathes, food, breath, and mental, are braided in our everyday experience. We're just moving, breathing, sensing, as if they were all one action. When we sit in meditation, however, concentrating our senses on the breath as it enters and leaves the body, the difference stands out. We become aware that the mind is not the breath is not the body. And we begin to notice more "us" out there, beyond body/breath/mind.

After the first three sheathes, Campbell tells us, there is a "big gap." We're beyond ordinary experience now. The everyday is behind us.

The fourth sheath, beyond the gap, is the *Vigyanmaya kosha*, or "wisdom sheath." Here's where things get interesting:

"This is the sheath of the wisdom of the transcendent pouring in. This is the wisdom that brought you to form in the mother's womb, that digests your dinners, that knows how to do it. This is the wisdom that, when you cut yourself, knows how to heal the wound. The cut bleeds, and then a scab comes along. Finally a scar forms. And this is the wisdom sheath going to work… This is the level of your Nature Wisdom, that you share with the hills, with the trees, with the fish, with the animals."

That "big gap" between body/breath/mind and this fourth, transcendent sheath, between the personal and the transpersonal, between knowledge and wisdom, between individual consciousness and the Collective Unconscious, is where mythology matters. Campbell writes that:

"The power of myth is to put the mental sheath in touch with this wisdom sheath, which is the one that speaks of the transcendent."

The mind communicates in words. Wisdom, which is beyond words, speaks in images. The wisdom sheath is the origin of dreams, myth, and religion. It's where we each personally connect with all that transcends the personal.

Mythology bridges the gap, bringing images and words together.

It's the language of the soul.

The fifth and final sheath is the *Anandamaya kosha*, or "bliss sheath." This is where we're personally connected to the unending, non-dual bliss every religion points toward.

But if we reject mythology, and confine ourselves to the everyday, scientific, *"technological"* side of the gap, forget about bliss. You can't get there from here.

The Power of Myth

To break away from *"the entire level of consciousness on which truly mythic experience was feasible,"* is to be separated from the transcendent. To be trapped in the body, the breath, the senses. Severed from wisdom.

The power of myth is the power to know your own soul, to unite the personal and the transcendent dimensions of its world.

Embrace myth. Learn to speak the soul's language.

"Myth is not the same as history; myths are not inspiring stories of people who lived notable lives. No, myth is the transcendent in relationship to the present." — Joseph Campbell

My Out of Body Experience
#OBE #ThisHappenedToMe

"I am more than my physical body. Because I am more than physical matter, I can perceive that which is greater than the physical world." — Robert Monroe, founder of The Monroe Institute

Vibrating Fire

I was nowhere "near death." But I *was* sick.

It was 1990. I was a college student sharing a house with a friend. Lori lived upstairs and paid most of the rent (she was not a student, and had a real job). I inhabited a finished room in the basement, for which I paid $80 a month. It was a sweet deal.

I'd gone to class that morning, but felt a bug coming on all day, getting worse as each hour passed. By the time my final class ended, I was running a fever and shiver-sweating profusely. I found my way home, downed two Tylenols, wrapped myself in blankets, and sank into the welcoming comfort of my bed. I was asleep in seconds.

This was around 4:00 PM.

A little after 5:00, Lori came home from work. Her dog, ecstatic to see her, woke me with a wild tap-dance on the kitchen floor above me. I found myself sitting on the edge of the bed. I stood, and took three long strides toward the stairway.

I felt strange. Every inch of my body, from the top of my head to the soles of my feet, was vibrating as if a strong electric current was passing through me. It didn't hurt, exactly, but it was intensely uncomfortable. It was similar to the feeling when you bump your funnybone. Hard. But the feeling was everywhere.

To access the stairs, I had to open a door. I reached for the knob, and my hand went right through. That's when I saw that my hand — and, I quickly realized, all of me — was made of *vibrating fire*. I was the shape of my body, I had hands and everything, but my "skin" was a coruscation of fiery reds and yellows.

I have to show myself to Lori, I thought. I knew I was Out of Body. I wanted verification. What would she see if I appeared before her?

The Golden Doorway

I couldn't open the door. I'd witnessed my hand passing right through the wood, so I don't know why it didn't occur to me to just walk through, full body. But it didn't. I turned, instead, toward the bed behind me. I was hesitant to look, because I felt intuitively that if I saw my body I'd be drawn back into it, and I didn't want the experience to end.

But my body lying there, wrapped in blankets and looking remarkably like a comatose stranger, turned out to be the least of my worries. A few feet past the foot of the bed, standing impossibly in the empty space of the room, was a large, rectangular doorway outlined in golden light. On the other side, through the door, I could see a lush, para-disiacal jungle, teeming with life. Birds screeched to one another in the trees, while crawling things scurried invisibly through the underbrush.

Intuition whispered: *"That way lies eternal happiness. And you're invited." All you have to do is walk through."*

But I was pretty sure if I accepted the offer, I'd be dead. My roommate would find my body, and that would be that. The thought of physical death scared the hell out of me (or heaven, as the case may be), and I was suddenly back in my body. I bolted upright in the bed, wide awake, sucking air in frantic gulps like a swimmer surfacing from deep water.

The doorway was gone, but the memory of it lingered. I could feel it there, slowly dissi-pating like a cloud before me.

I was glad I'd chosen life, but at the same time I was desperately sad.

I was also well. The fever was gone. My body felt golden, radiant, teeming with life.

Was it Just a Dream?

Skeptics will likely conclude my experience was a vivid dream. My arguments to the contrary are purely subjective, but I think they're worth considering.

First, I'd been recording and interpreting my dreams for years when the experience occurred. I was (and remain) intimately familiar with my dreaming mind. This was like no dream I had experienced before. No dream even vaguely like it has occurred in the almost three decades since. I know my dreams, and this did not "feel" like a dream.

Second, because of the way dreams work in the brain, we begin to forget them the moment we open our eyes. We rarely remember dreams long enough to write them down, let alone to recall them vividly decades later. I remember this experience in painstaking detail to this day. I can summon the exact feeling of that electrical vibration. I can see that doorway. Every detail of that room is etched in memory.

Was it a Lucid Dream?

"Lucid Dreaming is the scientifically proven ability to become 'self aware' in your dreams. This means you KNOW that you're dreaming and as such are able to control the dream, fly around, explore your mind and do whatever you can imagine." — Howtolucid.com

By no means did I *"know I was dreaming."* I was acutely self-aware during the experience, but with no reference to dreaming whatsoever. And I certainly couldn't *"control the dream, fly around..."* etc. I couldn't even open a door.

I'll go with Out of Body Experience.

How to Think About Gods

Are religious myths true or false?
It depends on where you stand.

How Most People Think About Gods

I've studied world religions, spirituality, and related topics for over forty years. Most of the people I've met along the way or whose books I've read fall into two broad groups:

People who believe the religion they practice is literally true, while everyone else's religion is based on myth, most charitably defined as *stories of gods and heroes which, while they may hold historical/cultural significance, are not literally true*.

and

People who don't practice any organized religion. The "spiritual but not religious" usually allow that the world's religious myths, while not literally true, can hold spiritual, moral, or psychological value. Atheists tend to consider all myths false and disposable, and sort them along a spectrum ranging from frivolous to dangerous.

Are You In? Or Are You Out?

In his Great Courses lecture series *Myth in Human History*, Professor Grant L. Voth makes this point regarding the relationship between religion and myth:

The first thing to be said about the relationship between religion and myth is that a myth can only be a myth if you don't believe it, if you stand outside of it in some kind of way. If you stand inside a myth, then it becomes something quite different. It becomes divine truth… Moses parting the Red Sea, or Jesus' resurrection, are clearly myths to Buddhists and Hindus. Mohamed's night flight to Heaven looks like a myth unless you happen to be a Muslim. Joseph Smith's discovery of the Golden Tablets looks like a myth unless you happen to be a Mormon. All of Vishnu's incarnations as Krishna look like a myth unless you happen to be Hindu. The fact that Buddha was born from his mother's side after his mother had a dream of a white elephant looks like a myth unless you happen to be Buddhist. Osiris begetting a child on Isis after he's already dead looks like a myth unless you happen to be inside it and believe it.

In philosophy, this is one dimension of *the Philosophical Problem of Religious Diversity*, which I've written about at length in previous essays.

The fresh idea I want to explore today is Professor Voth's concept of

standing *inside a myth*

and

standing *outside a myth.*

Look again at his observation that

"...a myth can only be a myth if you don't believe it, if you stand outside of it in some kind of way. If you stand inside a myth, then it becomes something quite different. It becomes divine truth..."

What if that's not a metaphor?

What if, when a Christian and an atheist argue regarding the resurrection of Jesus, *they might both be right?*

Because one is standing *inside the myth* and one is standing *outside the myth*?

For the Christian, standing inside the myth, the resurrection is literally true.

For the atheist, standing outside the myth, the resurrection is literally false.

And they're both right.

In and Out of Love

I hear the logicians screaming, *"It has to be one or the other! It can't be both!"*

But consider the same question, posed in a non-religious context.

Here's how the great Chilean poet Pablo Neruda describes love:

I love you as the plant that never blooms
but carries in itself the light of hidden flowers;
thanks to your love a certain solid fragrance,
risen from the earth, lives darkly in my body

.... so I love you because I know no other way

than this: where I does not exist, nor you,
so close that your hand on my chest is my hand,
so close that your eyes close as I fall asleep.

Then there's the scientific view, as described here by Megha Alcorn:

Love is a complex neurobiological phenomenon, relying on trust and belief as well as brain reward activity, i.e., limbic processes. These processes critically involve oxytocin, vasopressin, dopamine, and serotoninergic signaling. Moreover, endorphin and endogenous morphinergic mechanisms, coupled to nitric oxide autoregulatory pathways, play a role. Naturally rewarding or pleasurable activities are necessary for survival and appetitive motivation, usually governing beneficial biological behaviors like eating, sex, and reproduction.

So, which description is "true?" Who's right about love?

They both are.

Neruda is right, reporting from his position *inside love.*

Alcorn is right, looking at love *from the outside.*

How to Think About Gods

What if Deity works the same way — and this is the real meaning of *faith*?

What if faith is *standing inside the myth,* where the reality of God/Goddess/gods exists to be experienced?

What if, however deftly neuroscientists calibrate their fMRI scans, the reality of God/Goddess/gods will elude them *because they're looking in the wrong place —* **outside the myth?**

Oh ye of little faith!

Are religious myths true or false? It depends on where you stand.

Is God Imagination?

Not "imaginary," but imagination itself

Childhood's End

I remember the exact moment my childhood ended.

This is not a trauma story. At some point, childhood ends for everyone. Young adulthood begins. I just happen to remember the exact day that transition occurred, or at least the day I became aware of it.

It was the first day of summer break, between the 4th and 5th grades. For years, my sister and I had kicked off our summers playing "gas station." We'd set up a card table "convenience store" in the driveway, stocked with cans of soda and packs of candy cigarettes. The garden hose was the fuel pump. We'd take turns riding our bikes around the block, then pulling into the station. Whoever was the "driver," the other got to be the gas station attendant. The attendant filled the tank, cleaned the windshield, and checked the oil, while the driver enjoyed a relaxing smoke and listened to the radio, just like we'd seen adults doing all our lives.

It was fun — innocent, imaginary child's play. We never tired of it.

But that summer, things changed.

We set up the table as usual. My sister took off on her bike. I waited by the "pump," windshield rag at the ready, a pack of candy cigs nested in the rolled up sleeve of my t-shirt.

She rounded the corner and pulled into the station.

We looked at each other.

And felt ashamed.

She felt it. I felt it. We could see it in each other's reddening faces.

We were too old for this.

What if someone saw us? "Playing pretend" like little children?

We exchanged a few nervous words, put the card table away, and went our separate ways. I spent the rest of the day alone in my room, reading and quietly brooding over the experience.

We didn't turn overnight into somber adults, but from that day forward, "play" meant playing sports, card games, board games like Chess, Monopoly, or Risk. "Real world" games with rules, strategy, and competition. Games that *engaged* our imaginations, but didn't originate there.

Imagination, How Impaired and Restored

In *Natural Supernaturalism: Tradition and Revolution in Romantic Literature,* M. H. Abrams devotes his first 200 pages to analyzing William

Wordsworth's 8,000 line poem *The Prelude*—Books XI and XII of which are titled *Imagination, How Impaired and Restored*.

Let me briefly summarize, in 200 words, what Abrams expounds in 200 pages:

The Prelude, loosely patterned on Milton's *Paradise Lost*, is the poet's account of the development of his own creative imagination, from the playful immersion in fantasy of childhood, to the break with nature and surrender to sobriety that typifies adulthood, to his imagination's redemptive return in the higher form of *art* —in his mature, creative work as a poet.

Where Milton saw Adam's innocence, walking side by side with God in the Garden, Wordsworth saw the magic of childhood, of everyone's instinctive original identification with a natural world we only recently emerged from ourselves (the womb), and with all its sublime embodiments in the trees, birds, bugs, animals, mountains, rivers, wind, and weather around us.

Where Milton saw the Fall, and Adam's expulsion from Paradise, Wordsworth saw the demands of civilization that separate us from nature and thrust us into the responsible society of men. I read this to mean things like education, employment, money, marriage, family.

Where Milton saw Christ entering history to redeem fallen Humanity, Wordsworth saw *art* — creativity, the trained, inspired adult imagination — reconciling maturity and innocence, restoring our childhood exuberance, and reconnecting us on a higher level to the Divine Imagination from which we all emerge.

It would be easy to dismiss this scheme of the birth, death, and resurrection of imagination as poetic license, but Wordsworth takes the idea beyond metaphor. In his formulation:

the God who walked with Adam in the Garden IS the imagination that walks with everyone in childhood.

God *IS* the imagination crucified by education, work, responsibility.

God *IS* the imagination resurrected through art.

God is not *like* imagination.

God does not simply *inspire* imagination.

God *IS* imagination.

Wordsworth's identification of imagination with God was shared by other Romantic poets:

"This world of Imagination is the world of Eternity; it is the divine bosom into which we shall all go after the death of the... body. This world of Imagination is Infinite and Eternal... There exists in that Eternal World the Permanent Realities of Every Thing which we see reflected in... Nature. All things are comprehended in their Eternal Forms in the divine body of the Saviour, True Vine of Eternity, The Human Imagination." — William Blake

"The Primary Imagination I hold to be the living Power and Prime Agent of all human Perception, and as a repetition, in the finite mind, of the eternal act of creation in the infinite I AM." — Samuel Taylor Coleridge

Is God Imagination?

My own experience parallels *The Prelude*. I was expelled from the Paradise of innocence that long ago summer, but imagination never abandoned me. It sank underground throughout my teen years in a voracious appetite for reading, especially science fiction, and hooked itself tenaciously to anything in popular culture that left it room to breathe — religion, ghost stories, astrology, the New Age (I grew up mostly in the '70s). In my twenties, imagination called me to take up writing, and here I am today, crafting this very essay — evidence of my *"imagination's redemptive return in the higher form of art,"* of conscious, mature creativity.

Now, reread that paragraph, replacing the word *"imagination"* with *"God."*

The meaning is unchanged.

Most religions conceive of God (God, Goddess, gods, deity) as the Creator and Sustainer of reality.

Here are some things we know about imagination:

Neuroscience tells us that, while our brains don't create the physical world outside our heads, they do create and sustain 100% of *our experience of that world.* **We can never know the outside world directly, only our inner, mental (imagined) representation of it.**

Idealist philosophers suggest that, not just our inner representation, but the physical world itself, could be created and sustained by our minds.

We all know from experience that imagination creates and sustains whole worlds every night in our dreams.

Is God imagination? Is imagination God?

Don't rush to answer. Live with the question awhile.

Just imagine where it might take you.

God Killed the Great Mother.
Science is Dancing on Her Grave.
Let's Bring Her Back to Life and
Save the World.
What the World Needs Now
— Scientific Animism

"If we are to have any chance of surviving the looming catastrophe that science and technology have inadvertently helped to create we will need more wisdom, not more analytical capacity... We now urgently need to develop a new approach in science that integrates analysis with wisdom, fact with value, and nature with culture... by replacing our demonstrably unwise (and until recently, unconscious) assumption that the world is an inert machine with the arguably wiser and more accurate metaphor that the world is a vast animate (and hence 'sentient') being." — Stephan Harding, *Towards an animistic science of the Earth*

What is Scientific Materialism?

Webster's Dictionary defines *"Materialism"* as:

"A theory that physical matter is the only or fundamental reality, and that all being and processes

and phenomena can be explained as manifestations or results of matter."

Scientific Materialism is the corresponding assumption, within Science, *"that the world* [all reality] *is an inert machine"* to be taken apart, studied, and explained in exclusively physical terms.

In the view of Scientific Materialism, people, plants, animals, the Earth, the Moon, the Sun, planets, stars, galaxies — *all things* — are composed of "dead matter." The job of science is to explain by what equally-dead, mechanical processes all that dead matter came to hold its current form.

I've been listening to Professor Grant L. Voth's Great Courses lecture series *Myth in Human History*, which explores world mythologies from deep prehistory to the modern era. One thing that has become abundantly clear to me, following the mythological timeline, is that for most of the time human beings have existed, *nobody, anywhere on Earth, has understood the physical world to be composed of "dead matter."*

Materialism is a very new idea.

But not as new as you might think.

Science didn't invent it.

God Killed Matter

According to Professor Voth, there was a prehistoric span of around 25,000 years where the physical Earth was everywhere considered a living Goddess. Her names and stories varied by culture, but the core belief was universal. The Earth was the body of the Great Mother. All living things were born from her, and returned to her at death. Not only people, but everything that exists was born from her, and so everything that exists was alive.

The religious word for this is *Animism*. Wikipedia tells us:

> *Animism (from Latin anima, "breath, spirit, life") is the religious belief that objects, places and creatures all possess a distinct spiritual essence... animism perceives all things — animals, plants, rocks, rivers, weather systems, human handiwork and perhaps even words — as animated and alive... Animism predates any form of organized religion and is... the oldest spiritual and supernatural perspective in the world. It dates back to the Paleolithic Age, to a time when ... humans roamed the plains hunting and gathering, and communing with the Spirit of Nature.*

Starting around 3,000 BCE, Indo-European invaders, who had domesticated horses and camels, developed military technologies like the chariot, and envisioned male warrior sky gods who shared their martial values, conquered the older Mother Goddess cultures. Beliefs about how people and animals and mountains and rivers got here changed. In some places, the chief sky god killed the Great Mother and constructed the world from pieces of her dismembered body. In others, he fashioned the world from his own body, or from preexisting chaos, the way a craftsman assembles a finished product. The feminine metaphor of *"creation = birth"* became the masculine metaphor *"creation = making."* The Great Mother was demoted to consort, helper, or wife of the sky god. In this middle period came pantheons like the Greek, with Zeus and Hera, or the Norse, with Odin and Frigg.

Somewhere around 2,000 BCE, Monotheism began kicking the women out altogether. It declared that a single all-male God created everything, with no help from anybody. This last iteration is the only one most people know today. In Western Culture, the word "Religion" is nearly synonymous with "Monotheism."

The shift from pantheons of gods and goddesses to a monotheistic all-male God, *killed matter.*

Here's how Professor Voth explains it:

God has replaced the Goddess. The maker takes over the function of the one who gives birth... the deity is no longer immanent in the world. Rather, the deity shapes dead material into form, and that makes for a huge separation between subject and object. And the gap "kills" part of creation, by seeing it as something dead, something inert, something to be manipulated, rather than something sacred in itself because it issues from the body of the Goddess...

...the view that nature itself is sacred is sometimes called Animism, and in monotheistic religions it's a heresy. It's a leftover from pagan times. Since in those monotheistic religions, God is always thought of as outside of nature, as beyond nature, as detached from it. And therefore it is a heresy to find God inside nature in this kind of way.

In other words, *God killed matter.*

Materialism is a byproduct of Monotheism.

Which means Scientific Materialism is *Science clinging to 4,000 year old religious dogma.*

It's time for that to change.

Scientific Animism

So, what would a liberated, dogma-free, *Scientific Animism* look like?

Here's Stephan Harding, again from *Towards an animistic science of the Earth*:

So how can we bring together this long tradition of animistic thinking with our modern scientific understanding of the earth?

...we can conceive of matter as being inherently creative... much as an artist explores new domains of being and interaction. For animists, matter and psyche are indissoluble, for the psyche of the world resides nowhere else but in matter itself... in the very molecules and atoms that constitute our palpable, sensing bodies.

...we can no longer treat matter with disrespect, because it is, after all, sentient... We realise the profound wisdom in the etymological root of the word 'matter', which comes from the Latin for 'mother' (mater), and 'matrix', or womb.

Monotheism killed the Great Mother.

Science is dancing on her grave.

Scientific Animism could bring matter, the Goddess — *and Science* — back to life.

With a little luck, in time to avert *"the looming catastrophe that science and technology have inadvertently helped to create."*

In time to save her human children from themselves.

Life Squeezes the Soul
— Why We Crave Spirituality

A Jungian Look at the Big Human Picture.
There's more to you than meets the eye.

My mom always said my very first career goal, expressed at the tender age of six, was to be a preacher. I have no memory of the incident, but the story goes that I was so moved by some sermon the minister preached at the Methodist church I grew up in that I ran squealing to the lectern and, in front of the whole congregation, threw myself around his pant-leg, looked up dreamily, and declared, *"When I grow up I want to be a preacher, just like you!"*

By eleven, I was eagerly exploring (a kid version of) the major world religions, with a special interest in Buddhism. I soon tumbled headfirst into the New Age Movement, which was exploding in popularity around that time (the mid-1970s). Aspects of that eclectic spiritual subculture carried me into my twenties. In college, I minored in Comparative Religions.

In the course of my now 55 years, I've been a Protestant Christian, a SciFi atheist, a devotee of Carlos Castaneda's Toltec writings, a Gurdjeffian, an "armchair Rajneehsy" and an "armchair Buddhist" ("armchair" meaning I

92

read a lot of books in these disciplines without formally committing to them), a Catholic Christian, a Wiccan, and probably most of all, woven through and between all those apparently disparate threads, a self-styled mystic whose primary allegiance was always less to any specific religion or teaching than to a deep, existential passion for spirituality itself.

For the last five decades, while other people were doing practical things like living full, balanced lives, pursuing degrees that led to lucrative careers, and learning how to cook, program computers, and repair automobiles, I was chasing God in all His/Hers/Its/Their many guises.

Oh yeah. And somewhere in the midst of all that, in my mid-twenties through mid-thirties, I also invested a decade in a self-directed study of Jungian Psychology.

I'm not saying all this to brag. I'm qualifying myself to write the rest of this essay without a net.

That's the challenge I've set for myself today. I'm going to try to explain the attraction of spirituality, as I have come to understand the term, off the top of my head, without quoting famous people or linking to learned sources. I'll be coming at this from a Jungian perspective, but one admittedly skewed to support my own conclusions. My apologies in advance to Jungian purists.

I'm not advocating any one spiritual path here. I'm digging to expose the deep, human root that makes the pursuit of spirituality, by any path, such an urgent need for so many of us.

The Soul According to Jung (as Interpreted, and Very Possibly Misinterpreted, By Me)

According to Jung, embedded within all human souls are numerous primordial images, energetically-charged universal symbols. They are innate, inherited structures within the soul. They influence our thoughts, feelings and behavior, whether we're aware of them or not (mostly, we're not). Jung labeled these images *Archetypes*.

Archetypes are broad, universal patterns that manifest similarly in all humans everywhere. They're innate, which means that, while you will learn after your birth the forms in which your particular culture expresses archetypal imagery (in religion, ritual, drama, art, stories, etc.), you're born already possessing the capacity to recognize those expressions because the archetypes, in their raw, natural form, are already a part of you.

Some of the most commonly discussed archetypes include, on the masculine side, figures like the Father, the King, the Warrior, the Wise Old Man, the Hero, and the Magician, and on the feminine side, the Mother, the Queen, the Maiden, the Wise Old Woman, the Heroine, and the High Priestess.

There are dozens of archetypes, major and minor. This list is not meant to be exhaustive. I just want to get the basic the idea across.

What matters for this discussion is that, while many of the archetypes can be grouped into masculine and feminine expressions, *every human soul contains them all*. The soul of every person reading these words contains both a Father and a Mother archetype, a King and a Queen, a Magician and a High Priestess.

The human soul, according to Jung, is *androgynous*.

Life Squeezes the Soul
— Anima and Animus

To picture what happens to the soul in the course of a human lifetime, imagine a water balloon with the archetypes floating inside.

When you're born, the first judgment the outside world makes about you is whether you have male or female genitalia. Based on that one physical observation, your parents, other people, and all the institutions of society (your family, schools, churches, etc.) sort you onto either the "boy" or "girl" track of socialization.

Now picture a hand squeezing the middle of the balloon and forcing half the archetypes to flow toward the outside world (consciousness), while the other half get pushed away from it (relegated to the unconscious). If you are socialized as a girl, the feminine archetypes will be drawn to the front and center position. You'll be encouraged to forget the masculine archetypes even exist — *for you*. You'll be taught to recognize their expressions in the outside world — fathers, kings, warriors, etc. — but not in yourself. *"You can't be those things because you're a girl,"* society tells you.

If you're socialized as a boy, the same process occurs, only in reverse.

Ideally from the perspective of the larger culture (what society needs from you, and not necessarily what you need for yourself), at the end of the socialization process, the front and center gender-specific archetypes reach their developed conscious expressions, and the boy or girl will take their place in society as a mature man or woman. A "Good King" or "Good Queen."

Those opposite-gender archetypes aren't gone, though. They've just been banished to the unconscious, where they constellate together to form an opposite-sex personality, the Anima in men and the Animus in women, a mysterious and alluring dark man or woman you'll meet in your dreams and search for desperately in waking life. You'll project your Anima or Animus onto the real people you date, making them appear perfect and magical, made for you in every way... *for a while.* When the projection is eventually withdrawn and you see them for who they really are, you'll think, *What happened?*

The important takeaway so far is that, growing up, your androgynous soul endured a socialization process that split it in half. By adulthood you became a mature women or man in the world, with a primordial, energetically-charged opposite-sex personality hidden away in your unconscious.

Both of those personalities *are you.*

Life Sculpts the Soul — The Shadow

Let's talk about your conscious personality (in Jungian-speak, *Persona*). The one you're aware of. The one that isn't your Anima/Animus.

Your soul and your personality are not the same thing. Your soul is the "essential you" that existed before you were born. For those who believe in reincarnation (I do), your soul is the you that migrates from life to life.

Your personality is a mask that your soul acquires in each lifetime. Personality is a compromise between your essential self and what the outside world dishes out during the socialization process.

Where, before, you pictured the hand of socialization squeezing a balloon, now see that hand holding a chisel. Your soul is now a block of marble.

Growing up, life sculpts your personality. Aspects of who you really are that are accepted by your family, schools, churches, etc., are supported and become prominent. That marble gets polished. Aspects that are rejected by your family, schools, churches, etc. get chiseled away.

But as we saw with the opposite-gender archetypes, nothing in the psyche ever really "goes away." Instead, the parts of you that don't meet the world's expectations disappear into the unconscious.

Were you raised to believe *"boys don't cry?"* Your tears are in the unconscious. Were you taught *"girls must be passive?"* Your assert-iveness is in the unconscious. Was there a rule in your home that *"we don't express anger?"* Guess what. You're unconscious is raging.

All the parts of your essential self that your unique socialization experience declared un-acceptable got chiseled away and sent to fester in the unconscious. There, just as happened with the Anima or Animus, they constellated together into a personality — a pissed off, poorly-behaved you that Jung labeled the *Shadow*.

Your Shadow is the monster that chases you in dreams. It's the part of you that sabotages relationships and jobs. In many ways your Shadow acts on your life as your own personal Devil.

However, your Shadow is also a treasure room containing critical pieces of your essential self.

Your tears are not evil. Your assertiveness is not evil. Your anger is not evil.

Somebody just didn't like them, growing up. So you banished them to the unconscious.

In Marvel Universe terms, think of Bruce Banner, with The Hulk lurking inside him. Yes, The Hulk is angry. The Hulk is violent. The Hulk is uncontrollable when released. But The Hulk is also Bruce's superpower. He's the part of Bruce that can save the day. Get the job done. Win the fight.

The Hulk — the Shadow — is different in each of us because we all experienced different shaming and sculpting growing up. But we all have one. Our Shadow is the fierce guardian of all the parts of ourselves we had to give up to be accepted by the world.

Why We Crave Spirituality

When you started reading this essay, you probably just felt like you.

Now you're aware your "just me" has at least two hidden aspects (Anima/Animus, and Shadow) that share the stage with a huge cast of characters — the Father, the King, the Warrior, the Wise Old Man, the Hero, the Magician, the Mother, the Queen, the Maiden, the Wise Old Woman, the Heroine, the High Priestess, and many more.

You may not know yet what all this Jungian stuff adds up to, but one thing should by now be crystal clear:

There's more to you than meets the eye.

Pretty much all my life I could feel — in a way that's hard to quantify, but if you've read this far I'll bet you know exactly what I mean — that the "me" I saw in the mirror, the me out to please parents and teachers, that fawned on ministers, that was learning things in school and church, that struggled to be accepted, was only the tiniest tip of the iceberg of who I really was. The world treated me as an ordinary kid in a plain small town, but I experienced myself to be vast inside.

As Walt Whitman phrased it in his poem *Song of Myself:*

"I am large, I contain multitudes."

My study of Jungian Psychology put words and concepts to that feeling. It wasn't just me; it was everybody. We are all so much more than what we see in the mirror.

Most of us, I think, are sooner or later shaken by the dissonance between our routine lives, our mundane selves, and the undeniable vastness we feel inside. All spiritual systems I'm aware of consist, at least in part, in tools — meditation, prayer, rituals, spiritual exercises — designed to assist in accessing that vastness, in reintegrating the split-off pieces of ourselves, in *Living Large*.

Jung called that reintegration process, and its goal, *Individuation*. To be individuated is to be whole. Complete. It's what every human longs for.

Spirituality provides paths to wholeness, to individuation. And that's why we crave it.

By this definition, Jungian Psychology would itself qualify as a spirituality, and I wouldn't argue. That's certainly been the role it has played in my life.

A Closing Thought About Religions

It's trendy these days to despise organized religions. That's understandable, based on the bad behavior of some religious adherents, but I think there's a larger perspective worth considering.

Many people these days see spirituality and religion as two different things. Some even consider them contradictory opposites.

But my experience has been that when you align the edges just right, spirituality and religion can be made to fit together neatly, like a pair of nesting dolls.

As explored in this essay, I believe spirituality is how individuals respond to awareness of the vastness inside, and the *"primordial images, energetically-charged universal symbols"* — archetypes — that reside there.

Religions, in my view, while differing in the details, universally declare that outer reality, too, is vast, and filled with *"primordial images, energetically-charged universal symbols"* — gods, goddesses, angels, devils, devas, faeries, nature spirits, etc.

Human reality reflects Divine reality. As above, so below. The line between inner space and outer space is at best arbitrary, and may be nonexistent.

That's the Human Big Picture. IMHO.

Connect with Jack Preston King

Author website:
jackprestonking.com

Medium:
medium.com/@jackprestonking

Twitter:
twitter.com/JackPrestonKing

Facebook:
facebook.com/authorjackprestonking

Made in the USA
Middletown, DE
07 August 2023